Deep Within

CONVERSATIONS with GOD

Ginny Sorrentino & Ryan Slodyczka

Deep Within

CONVERSATIONS with GOD

Ginny Sorrentino & Ryan Slodyczka

Harp & Sword
MEDIA

Deep Within: Conversations with God by Ginny Sorrentino and Ryan Slodyczka
Copyright © 2026. All rights reserved.

Published by Harp & Sword Media LLC
129 S. Main St., #260
Grapevine, TX 76051
www.harpandswordmedia.com

Cover and interior design by YOUNG DESIGN, LLC | youngdesignportfolio.com

Scripture quotations are taken from The Holy Bible, New International Version®, NIV®. Copyright © 1973, 1978, 1984, 2011 by Biblica, Inc. Used with permission of Zondervan. All rights reserved worldwide. www.zondervan.com

No part of this publication may be reproduced, stored in a retrieval system, or transmitted in any form or by any means—for example, electronic, photocopy, or recording—without prior written permission of the publisher. The only exception is brief quotations in printed reviews.

ISBN (hardcover): 979-8-9988032-1-5
ISBN (ebook): 979-8-9988032-2-2

10 9 8 7 6 5 4 3 2 1

Printed in the United States of America

Dedicated to all who are searching for peace and joy from deep within.

Introduction

*G***inny:** On September 3, 2004, at 4 a.m., my Lord woke me and instructed me to get up and let the Holy Spirit flow through me on paper. Confused but obedient, I sat in my prayer chair and began my poetry journey from my heart. My prayer is that whoever touches these pages will be blessed deep within their heart and soul.

He wakens me morning by morning,
> wakens my ear to listen like one being instructed.

The Sovereign LORD has opened my ears (Isaiah 50:4–5).

*R***yan:** In early 2024, I was sitting in a small group meeting at church. The lesson began, and it was about the parable of the talents. To be honest, I've never enjoyed this parable— perhaps because I often relate most to the not-so-wise servant who did nothing with his talent. So that day, I found myself staring out the window and my mind adrift. But shortly after, I heard God say, "You have been told you can write, and you have done nothing with it." I was shaken. From that point forward, I did my best to be obedient, and Ginny was instantly on my heart to be a part of this project. This book is a product of obedience, and I pray it touches whoever holds and reads it. May our God have all the glory.

I Do Release

Help me, Lord, to hear Your voice in all I say and do
And let me know that all I am is just because of You
You are my Strength, my Guide, my Friend, my Comfort
And my Peace
So once again, I give to You
My all, I do release.

G.S.

Her Sweet Face

How sweet her face looked when she left
Her long hair pulled back and tied.
I wanted to lie down next to her and hold her as if she cried.
Her sick little body was ever so still as hours just slipped away.
It was then I knew all I could do was go to my knees and pray.
I asked God to welcome her in His arms as her breath became
Shallow and deep.
He confirmed to me that my loved one will be by His side in
His Tender keep.

G.S.

I Call, I Pray, I Give

I call upon Your name this day, as I so often do
I pray my faith would always grow
As I give my all to You
I've seen how You can make a way
When doors close one by one
You are my All in All, dear Lord
My confidence You've won.

G.S.

Help Me

Help me to show them Your grace and Your love
And point them to You, Dear Lord, up above
Help me to tell them how full they can feel
When they bask in Your presence and pray as they kneel
Help me to love with compassion so sweet
And to see through Your eyes the people I greet
Help me to always help others see You
In my face and my words
And in all that I do.

G.S.

I Knelt

When I finally knelt at His bloodstained feet
I knew my Lord was whom I'd meet
I felt His tears upon my face
Flowing from His forgiving grace
How did I stay away so long
From the One who makes me bold and strong?
For in salvation I can see
How Jesus Christ has set me free.

G.S.

Indescribable

Resting in Your arms
Breathing in Your presence
Everything wanes away
There is not a blemish of worry
Nor a moment of fright
For fear of the Lord brought me here
Resting
The days grow long
The debts feel high
But when worship is my song
I know it was You all along
The yearning
The desire
The emptiness in our being
Is not filled by anything
But God.

As I rest in this quiet place
I am filled beyond my language
For whom can describe You?

R.S.

Faith of a Bird

As daylight comes, I hear the sounds of singing soft and sweet
It makes me smile and think of God, whom one day I shall meet.
These little birds are quite a gift of such great thought and love
Their beauty was designed by our Creator up above.
I watch them perch and rest and eat with bellies plump and round
They have no cares for what comes next, for their supplies abound.
They have no thought for their next day of food or where they'll sleep
They simply trust and live their lives
While God controls their keep.

G.S.

Our Savior

We have a Savior who's faithful and true
His love and compassion are real
He seeks and He saves the wandering soul
and gives him the ointment to heal
Just come to the cross for forgiveness and rest
and give yourself unto the King
He'll fill you with power and hope and great strength
And give you a reason to sing.

G.S.

Trust Like a Whitecap

I see the whitecaps fighting on their journey to the shore
They're up and they're down, but they struggle for more
They know there's a place where their journey will land
So it's toward level ground that sparkles with sand
I pray that this time allows me to be
Just like those whitecaps way out in the sea
Trusting in God to bring me to shore
Just like the whitecaps that struggle no more.

G.S.

The Beach

As I arrive at the beach
The seagulls say hello
They make their joyous cawing sounds
Between the ebb and flow
They make me feel so welcome
And show me where to rest
I sit beneath God's pretty blue sky
And gaze upon His best
This is my place where I drink Him in
And pray and praise His name
He fills me with His love and grace
And THIS is why I came.

G.S.

Once Again

Once again, I sit alone
wondering what to do
I'm in a place that makes me sad
for all that I've been through
At times I ask my God above
what is my purpose here
He says His grace is good enough
To dry my every tear.

G.S.

A Call

Let not your hands grow weary
For the Lord of lords has personally redeemed you
And yet you say
"Now I rest"
"I am tired"
"I see no fruit"
Where were you when God measured the mountains in His hands?
Where were you when there was emptiness over the still waters?
Where were you
When God made you?
He reached down and saved you
What does God ask but for you to do the same?
Reach, my brother
Reach, my sister
Grab deep in your bag

And throw the seed as far as your being can
Look to the sun
Look to the wind
Who are we to say my time to rest is now?
Our Father is at the door
I say it again
I say it once more
Throw your seed
Spread the gospel with every might you can
The glory of God is present
Right in your hand.

R.S.

Peace and My Lord

I love the peace He gives to me
When I sit alone right by the sea
As my feet rest in the sand
My Lord just holds me by my hand
The sunny breeze is my best friend
I pray this time will never end
I'll sit and bask in His sweet love
As it pours on me from up above.

G.S.

Whisper Jesus

If you have eyes so weary and red because of tears and woe
I know a name that you can whisper so sweet, so soft, so low.
He'll calm your storms and dry your eyes with gentleness and love
He'll fill you with His healing power and blessings from above.
Just whisper, "Jesus," and be assured that He is in control
He will hear your every cry
And peace will flood your soul.

G.S.

Bird in My Tree

Sing to me, oh bird so high
Don't just perch there
Please don't fly!
Bless me with your gift of song
So I'll remember all day long
Your sweet, sweet sounds that comfort me
And how God placed you in my tree.

G.S.

The Cross

How wonderful a man was He
The One who bled and died for me
His mission was to save my soul
So I'd be gracefully made whole
My mission is to let you know
That to the cross is where you go
For pardon, peace, and healing love
And mercy drops from up above.

G.S.

Alone

Alone is where my mind must go
alone is where I'll be
That's when my God and I will meet
right there beside the sea
He'll take me to that place of peace
and lead me by the hand
He'll say, "Child, won't you lean on Me?
It's then I'll help you stand.
So come away and be with Me.
We'll sit and pray awhile.
It's at that time you will feel
your heart begin to smile."

G.S.

Righteous Man, Part 1

Where are you, oh righteous man?
The bells have clanged
The dinner is done
You begin to head home
Yet there is none
Where are you, oh righteous man?
You woke up today
To give yourself what you need
An endless greed, an endless greed
Where are you, oh righteous man?
Your sons and daughters
Shall be a special breed
Broken homes creating broken homes
But who's to care
When you don't see their stare?
Their eyes bleed the pillows

Their beds are wet from fear
Where did you go dad, where did you go?
I used to wait by the door
To hear what was in store
I used to wait by the phone
Until it never rang
You pick up and take off
Leaving nothing but the dirt off
Nobody said this would be easy
Nobody called to say goodbye
Yet when you took off
Whispers of your love
Breathed a lie
For love is not the selfish emotion
That stole you away
No
Love is a position of servitude
Love is humbling
Love is ever-enduring
Love is relentless
Amidst the storms and trials
Amidst the pain and denials
It's love that holds on
Love that endures forever
But selfishness burns a disaster
Your sons and daughters
Need you
They don't need a stepdad

They don't need a co-parent
A divorced plan
A copilot
They need a righteous man
To stand up and push forward
Repent
Believe in the gospel
Hold on to God, and He will hold on to you
Oh righteous man
You were right there all along
Have some faith
Listen to the song
God has called you all along
Fight for it
With all your might!
Go home
Embrace your wife
Father your children
Oh righteous man
Oh righteous man
Don't make your bed in sin
Look to Him
Look to Him
Then father them
As He loves you
Love unto them.

R.S.

One Day

One day our Jesus we shall see, His face so full of love.
He'll tell us, "No more weeping, child, here in My heaven above."
It's then when we will praise and sing and gaze forevermore
upon our Jesus' tender face—we'll worship and adore.
So one day in His arms we'll be, content and so secure
And feel His love so tender, so perfect, and so pure.

G.S.

Pink and Blue

If I could sit with them once more as Moms so often do
I'd tell them they are special gifts wrapped up in pink and blue.
I'd read and play, hug and kiss, love and cuddle them so much
And share with them my God above, about His tender touch.
My prayer for all the Moms out there is simple and it's true
Just ask for precious time to spare
For those in pink and blue.

G.S.

My Need for You

I need to be on my knees at Your feet
To feel Your touch and make me complete
Help me, dear Lord, to be less of me
So my life would be pleasing only to Thee.

G.S.

Me and My Lord

I love sitting outside early in the day
Just me and my Lord and my time to pray
I thank Him for flowers and trees all around
And birds that bless me with beautiful sound
And then I look up with a big, pleasing sigh
And say, "Thank You, Lord, for Your beautiful sky!"

G.S.

My Hidden Mask

Now and then I put it away
I thought it would stay in that place
But all of a sudden, my tears start to flow
It's time to cover my face
This mask is my friend I didn't ask for
God knew my need would arise
He gave me a mask just made for me
A mask that is just the right size.

G.S.

Righteous Man, Part 2

Righteous man
Where are you?
Your God calls
Yet you do not respond
Your God calls for repentance
Yet you do not hear
He reveals Himself
Each and every day
Yet you do not see
Drunk in flesh
The ransom has been paid
Yet your cashing is delayed
Who has mastered you, young man?
Who has made you their slave?
You have been set free!
Yet you flee

Running to the addictions of your flesh?
You ask for a test
Yet you have not a pen nor paper
Just the heartbeat for another favor
Broken promises
Broken families
You seek the world
For what's already in store
Search within your soul
The kingdom of God is here
The kindling's begun
The world ablaze
Yet you've not a taste?
His love is beyond measure
We cannot comprehend the magnitude of God
How can we hold a cup to this?
He is just and true
A Father we have always had
This world can shake you
And make you sad
Through and through
Hear me, please
Fear Him alone
Revere Him and seek Him
And He will dwell within you
And you will begin to see what is true
Let His Spirit lift you now!
Rise up!

Rise up out of the darkness
Rise up out of the desert
Seek God
The Lord of lords
Do not set your flesh in stables of misery
Your soul cries out
Yet you do not hear it under the blankets of comfort
Your physical being has warped your soul
One must go, one must go.

R.S.

Your Peace

I love when Your peace fills me in every way
At times when I need it the most
Just as for the birds in the air
You are my most honored Host
You know my needs before I ask
How could this love be mine?
I'm humbled in Your presence, Lord
And give thanks You're my True Vine.

G.S.

His Presence

When I close my eyes in faith, I pray
For God to meet me there
It's in His presence where I feel
His love when I'm in prayer
Oh, let me always praise You, Lord
When I am in that place
For Your unending, caring ways
And Your Amazing Grace!

G.S.

As I Am

As I am, I come again upon Your Holy Ground
With yet another plea for You, where true love shall abound
Help them to know that You're their God
Who gives such strength and love
And all they need to do is look to Thee in heaven above
For as I am, I pray they'll be submitted to You, Lord
So we can be a family and praise in one accord.

G.S.

This Blessed Hour

As dawn now comes at this blessed hour
I gaze upon Your mighty power
The sea so large, so active, yet still
Gives me peace, for I know my sad heart You will fill
For I know that You hold me and gather my tears
And this place I'm now in will be rid of its fears
You are my Strength, my Peace, my Strong Tower
My thirst has been quenched at this blessed hour.

G.S.

My Journey

Dear Lord, there's a path I have not traveled as yet
I ask that You show me the way
I know You can light up that road just for me
So I'll get on my knees, and I'll pray
I have faith that Your Word is a lamp for my feet
I can start my new journey today
One step at a time with You by my side
The Truth, the Life and the Way.

G.S.

Coming Home

How quickly we forget yesterday
How God moved in your life
What He did in your soul
To whom does that glory befall
If you forget to speak or tell at all?
Where is your fight, oh mighty warrior?
My ears listen for the horn
Yet there's none to be found
You stowed it away for another day
Yet the Lord of lords is at your door
Waiting to come in
Not prepared for the midnight thief
Oil lamp empty
You have got to be kidding me
Every line in Scripture, a promise kept and secured
Every line in Scripture, a prophecy fulfilled

Where are you, oh mighty warrior?
Where is your steed?
God did not call you to lie in bed
With not much life, mistakenly dead
Rise in the name of the Lord
Rise to the sound of the horn
Rise for the glory of the Lord
It is a testament to the new
To the old
And to the kingdom come
My God has come home

R.S.

Look to Me

Why do we search for a heartwarming love
When Jesus says, "Just look to Me"?
His love is warm, long-lasting, and real
All we would want it to be.
So look to the One who loves us the most
For peace, for comfort, for rest
And ask Him into your heart this day
Where He will be your best!

G.S.

Love of the Lord

Good morning, Lord, I feel Your love
Pouring down from above
I feel Your favor all around
It's leading me to a whole new ground
I trust You more and more each day
And rest in Your arms as I
Follow Your way.

G.S.

Help Them See

Oh, that I could help them see
How You loved them so much when You died on that tree
How the color of crimson made a way for their soul
And washed them so clean and made them whole.
If only the world would take hold of the King
Their burdens would be lighter, and then they would sing
Of the love of a Savior so deep and so pure
And compassion and grace they will know—this, I'm sure.

G.S.

Rest and Be Still

So much of this life leaves pain in our heart
It saddens us down to our core.
We look up to God and ask,
"How can this be?
I don't want to hurt anymore."
God says, "Do not waver like the wind of the sea
Pushing the waves to and fro.
Just rest and be still; trust in Me
And My peace will then overflow."

G.S.

Love and Grace

If I could see tomorrow
I'd know about my sorrow
My faith and trust would grow so weak
Knowing in my heart it's You I must seek
I thank You for Your love and grace
That always keep me in that place
Of comfort, joy, calm, and peace
Again to You, I do release.

G.S.

The Pit

Even if all else fails
Even if You keep me in the lions' pit
Even if the enemies circle around and end it all
Even if I can't breathe
Even if health deteriorates
Even if my bank runs dry
Even if all else fails
My love for You
My longing for You
Still churns onward through the choppy seas
My heart is set on You, my Father
Lest You forget Your servant in this land
Lest You forget me, my Father
Bring me home when the task You laid before me
Is complete and no more
My Father, keep Your Spirit within me

Let not the kingdom of God leave me
In the mighty name of Jesus Christ, amen.

R.S.

God's Sweet Love

I know You sent this hummingbird
To gaze into my eyes
For when I sat in morning prayer, I looked up with surprise
There he was with fluttering wings, right in front of me
Once again, You showed me how sweet Your love can be.

G.S.

Our Place

Here I sit again, Lord, in our peaceful place
Early morning talks with You
fill me with such grace
Again You send a hummingbird, so pretty and so small
and then You send a cottontail bouncing like a fluffy ball
Your presence gets more real to me as every day goes by
I love You, Lord, with all my heart
and that I won't deny.

G.S.

God Said

I heard a new but familiar sound
Everywhere I turned and looked around
It gave me breath down in my soul
It soothed my heart and made me whole
"It's peace like a river," God said to me
"Now go and enjoy and be all you can be."

G.S.

New Mercy

God's mercy and blessings are new every morning
He refreshes us every day
He opens our eyes and fills us with hope
And equips us in every way
But when we feel lonely and empty inside
And need to be filled once again
Just whisper, "Jesus," the name above all
And follow it with your "Amen."

G.S.

His Arms

My mind and my heart go to heaven's shore
When I sit by myself with my Lord
I feel like I'm floating on sun-kissed waves
As He rocks me back and fore
His arms hold me tight—they never let go
I feel so safe and secure
He says, "Look to Me—don't turn away
My love for you is pure."

G.S.

Finish

I see your pain
I feel your heartache
Continue on, young man
Follow the plan
Life's not easy
No one said it would be
Loving others first
Is not the curse
That the enemy whispers
Push onward, young man
When I meet you at the gates
What will we say?
I pray, I pray
"Well done, My good and faithful servant."
"Well done, My good and faithful servant."

R.S.

Time with My Lord

I love my time with You, my Lord
There's silence all around
You fill my mind with thoughts of You
And gratitudes abound
You are my Strength, my Peace, my Light
My Bright and Morning Star
I know when You are by my side
You guide me near and far.

G.S.

Get Closer

Dear Precious Lord, my Savior and King
I lean on Your promises, so to You I bring
A heaviness way down deep within
Its weight brings me sorrow
Please help me begin
Begin on this road to get closer to You
And never give up till my time here is through.

G.S.

In My Heart

God's blessings leave me speechless
My heart just overflows
There's so much I would like to say
But only my God knows
Oh Holy Spirit, tell me how
To speak what's in my heart
So others may be blessed this day
And make a brand-new start.

G.S.

Look and See

As I look out this window
Such beauty I can see
Mountains and trees all around
God says, "Lift up your eyes to Me
I made this for you.
Come ask Me for help
That's all you need to do.
Just know I am here right by your side
To love you and fill you
And always provide."

G.S.

Gifts of Color

Leaves of different colors
Yellow, red, orange, and brown
Such beauty to behold
I watch them graciously falling down
God speaks to me in such a way
His gifts to us cause me to pray
So as I watch them travel oh so gracefully
They dance and twirl and float around
Until they land to bless the ground.

G.S.

And He Heard

Where are You, Lord?
They encircle me
Trapping me on all sides
Anger and venom
Spitting on me
All around me
I cannot breathe
Their tongues whip around
I hear no sound
Only the whip of obscenity
My Lord, do not forsake me
My righteous Father
I am distraught
I have no friends in this place
The world comes after me
I have no peace in this broken land

It is sinking
All around me
My footsteps waver, slip, and slide
I'm just trying to get to You
Where are You? Please, my Lord
Please.
Rescue my soul
Rescue me from this land
It is a wretched place
The enemy shouts, screams, and kicks
Yet my God, it is You who sticks
I know it is You, but I can't seem to find You
My peace, Lord—please don't keep Your Spirit from me
Please keep Your Holy Spirit within me
Meet me, my God
Meet me where I lie
I need You now
My tears fall for You
My heart longs for You
O my God.
I feel so alone.

I hear You again
I feel Your presence
I feel Your warmth
Thank You, Lord
Invite me in again
Keep me safe again

O my God
How I long to be home
I am so distraught
I am mocked at and laughed at
The world does not choose me
Please always hold me
Keep me in Your hands
Lest Your Spirit depart from me
I will die, my Lord
I am a wretched man
Apart from You, I can do nothing
Apart from You, I am nothing
Set my heart on You
Set my soul ablaze for You
For whom can speak of such things?
For whom can describe what You are?
My Lord, my Lord, if I am to be here anymore
Light the furnace of my soul
Making You my only goal
I am dressed for duty
Fit for Your service
Though others speak ill of me
It is You, my Father
Within me
Sanctify me in truth
Let us not stumble over lies
Our Savior, Christ
Has made us perfect in Your eyes

We walk onward and forward
Strength beyond our flesh
Victory has happened
I attest I attest
My God, my God, light Your kingdom on fire
Making it my only desire
Making it my only desire!
We are all slaves in this world
I ask You to be my Master
Strip me naked of my broken desires
Lest I grow weary in pursuit of You
There lies no greater.

2 Corinthians 4:16–18

Lord, come and save me
God, bless those who seek You
For You are true
You are true
Thank You
My God, take all the glory
You just met me
Where I lay
As I turned to look at You
Your Kingdom is here to stay.

R.S.

Kneel and Pray

Lord, help our land to kneel and pray
So many people are going astray
Our minds are racing oh so fast
We need to know that this can't last
Our hearts are filled with strife and fear
Please help us feel that You are near
Open our eyes so we can see
All our land is supposed to be.

G.S.

God's Gifts

As I watch the sun go down
Colors and beauty all around
God is giving so much joy
Nothing and none could ever destroy
This huge bright ball of glowing yellow
Slowly disappears
It's sad to see it go away
At times it brings me tears
God promises He'll send it back
This great big ball of fire
To give us light and warmth and peace
And all that we desire.

G.S.

God Knows

As I reflect on the life I've had
I can see the ups and downs
So many twists and turns appear
So many causes for frowns
I also can see a power and strength
Loving and guiding me
I walk in His presence and look to His light
As He shows me all I can be.

G.S.

Your Blessings

There are so many ways You speak to me
And show me the way I should go
You bless me with treasures and pleasures to see
One by one, they just flow
I remember them all and picture each one
As I rest in Your love when my day is done.

G.S.

Blessings at Christmas

I love to sit and think of all my Christmas memories
So many lights and colors amid the many trees
My family circle was so big as we held hands to pray
We gave thanks to our Mighty God
On this most awesome day
I pray you all find love and joy
As you celebrate this little boy
Merry Christmas.

G.S.

Matthew 11:29-30

To whom do I declare my love
To whom do I speak of such things
Oh, where shall I go
When I don't quite know where to begin

Who formed me in my mother's womb
Who saw me for what I was to become
My Lord, my Lord

Oh, how I ponder the days of my existence
Oh, how I wonder where I am meant to be

But my Lord has cast light on my doubts
For I belong as I am
I am meant to be currently

My Lord, my Lord
Where shall I cast my burdens
My Lord, my Lord
Oh, how heavy they must be

But I hear oh so quietly
In my innermost being
Give them to Me

On my knees I cry
I look to the sky
Seeking peace
And forgiveness
I feel the weight release
Such peace, such peace

I stand up, exalting my God
Who formed me
Just for this time
And one day
One day soon
I will be home
But for right now
He's making more room
So bring everyone you can

The enemy's lies drown you
Yes, they can

But let the Spirit of the Lord
Conquer them all
As He has all authority
All in All

There is nobody
Like my Jesus
Nobody at all.

R.S.

Comfort and Joy

Fill me, Lord, with love and joy
At this special time of year
I pray for sadness and for loss
For healing to appear
Our hearts and minds travel many a place
We think of loved ones gone
We ask for Your compassion, Lord
Please comfort us this dawn
Help our minds to focus
On You, the real reason
For the gift of blessing us
With this very special season.

G.S.

An Ode to Jimmy Brown

I love my friend called Jimmy Brown
He always made me laugh
He loved the Lord and served Him well
And did it whole, not half
He's now an angel smiling down
That's my dear friend Jimmy Brown.

G.S.

Our Shore

The New Year is upon us; it's time to kneel and pray
And tell God how He's touched our lives
There's so much we could say
Let's tell Him how we love Him and pray to trust Him more
And ask for His forgiveness as we travel to our shore
Our shore is when our life is done and we see Him face-to-face
And glory in His presence as we bask beneath His grace.

G.S.

My Season

My heart is so full of my love for You
This season of life is so brand-new
I think of the times when I wandered around
As You led me through paths and so much I found
I found more and more how You take care of me
Just like the birds way up in the tree
O Lord, once again, I pledge all my love
As I open my eyes to You up above.

G.S.

I Pledge

Help me, Lord, to love You more and always put You first
And realize it's only You for whom I hunger and I thirst
You are my Rock, my One Strong Tower
Who holds me up with such great power
So unto You I pledge again
My love, my life, my all. Amen.

G.S.

Yahweh

Glory to Yahweh
To whom do I tell of what You have done
To whom do I whisper what You have whispered
You are the Almighty
You are the great I Am
When I was so lost
I was found
When I was hurting
You were waiting
Your restoration knows no limits
Your grace destroys borders
Your peace intercepts the lowest of depths
I did nothing to deserve this grace
Yet You pour
You pour it all over
Glory
To Yahweh.

R.S.

O Holy Spirit

I've been on roads that gave me joy
And then the enemy came to destroy
I'm sure he laughed when I was down
But he can never steal my crown
Again I come against this thief
O Holy Spirit, sigh of relief!

G.S.

Remember the Dash

Time has passed, and the stone is now placed
On the grave of the one that I lost
It states these two years—a birth and a death
It's neatly and crisply embossed
I know what it says, but all I can see
is the line that is carved in between
My eyes open wide, my heart sees it too
I feel so blessed and serene
The "dash" says it all—its story is real
It has all the smiles and tears
My memories come clear of this wonderful life
That was here for so many years.

G.S.

You Amaze Me

Lord, how You amaze me when I ponder all You do
You shine Your light, make a way, and always pull me through
You take me to such places, way deep inside my heart
Their names are peace and joy and love
Oh, what a place to start
This journey is exciting as I follow You each day
I know for sure You're always there to guide and show the way.

G.S.

Your Presence

In my loneliness, I know You are with me
I feel Your warm presence surrounding my heart
I cry out to You, Lord, to help me and guide me
And show me the way to a brand-new start
Please open my eyes to see this new road
The one I will follow with You to behold.

G.S.

Save Me, Show Me

I cry out to You, Lord
Save me from harm
As I walk through my life
I need Your strong arm
To lead me and guide me
And show me the way
The way is with You, Lord, and this I will pray
I'll pray that You'll take me by my hand
As You show me the way to Your promised land.

G.S.

Forgiveness

Forgiveness
Oh, forgiveness
Where have you gone?
Who has hidden you away?
The light that once shined
Has been tucked away
Spoken of another day
Oh, forgiveness, where have you gone?
Time is fleeting
It has left your very hands
You speak of today
Yet it's already gone away?
Oh, forgiveness
Let me hear your song
You hold it back
For what cause?

For who to win
You?
You're withholding the very thing
That would save you!
Oh, forgiveness
Oh, forgiveness
What a wonderful song
I see God's hand in it
All along
Listen and you will hear it
Heaven's been declaring it
Jesus Christ, the King of kings
Came down and saved us all
What a price He paid
So many attempts had been made
Finally, God stepped in to save
Now do the same
Forgive and move on
Wait for the Lord
Listen for the Holy Spirit
He will guide you through it
Forgiveness, forgiveness
Oh, what a wonderful song

R.S.

Who Am I?

How do I deserve all You do for me?
Who am I that You are mindful of all I am to be?
All I need is all You are
For You're my Bright and Morning Star
I seek Your face so I can hear
And know You'll wipe my every tear
You are my friend, my strength, my guide
I'm blessed to have You by my side.

G.S.

Gratitude

Today's a day to pray and praise
To You, my God, my hands I raise
My heart explodes with gratitude
As I sit here in my solitude
You open doors that fill my heart
And You close the ones that help me start
To once again renew my love
As comfort fills me from above.

G.S.

My Anchor

Oh Lord, You are an anchor for my soul
It's You alone who makes me whole
You are my Bright and Morning Star
My Ancient of Days who is never far
One day when we are face-to-face
I'll rest in Your arms and be full of Your grace.

G.S.

Sweet Sleep

I will lie down in peace when my day is done
I'll rest in my Lord till I see the sun
He promises me that my sleep will be sweet
So I won't be afraid—my day is complete
I'll wake and look up and thank Him for grace
I'll trust Him again and give Him all praise.

G.S.

Grace, Trust, Rest

Sometimes my path is lonely and sad
My heart feels broken; I want what I had
My God says, "My grace is sufficient for you."
Lord, help me to trust
That's all I can do
I'll rest in Your arms, so big and so strong
I know that's the place where I belong.

G.S.

Wait for the Lord

Like a breath of fresh air,
Flowing along the land,
Your gentleness
Holds us in Your hand.
As I stir and wake,
It is You, my Lord,
Who sits in wait.

R.S.

Help Me

Help me to love others as You have loved me
Help me to know how You want me to be
Let Your ways be my ways in all that I do
I need Your sweet guidance to help me get through
Your love is so big, I cannot perceive
But one thing's for sure
In You, I believe.

G.S.

I Know

Dear Lord, when I am in need of correction
I know Your love will draw me near
I trust that You will show the way
And I'll have nothing to ever fear
When I'm in need of comfort
I know Your Spirit will tell
He'll put His arms around me
As He whispers, "It is well."

G.S.

Sweet Spirit

O Holy Spirit, please give to me
All that You know will help me to see
Your love and Your guidance as I hear You say
"This is the life, the truth, and the way."
Fill me afresh with Your Spirit so sweet
As I look to the day my Savior I'll meet.

G.S.

Praise

Lift my head, O Lord, I pray
I fix my eyes upon You
Help me to focus on this precious day
And all that You will do
Help me to know Your mercy and grace
And to always remember how You died in that place
You are my Rock and my Strong Tower
I give my all to You this very hour.

G.S.

Sad

I spent some time with a beautiful robin
I believe it was her last day
My heart was sad; I felt so bad as I watched her pass away
I asked my Lord to help her through this one last task today
I'm sure her life blessed all who saw her beauty every day.

G.S.

Onward

Why do we rush so hastily unto death?
Our feet above the ground
Missteps along the way
Our gratefulness forgotten for today
Stop
Slow down
Meditate on His Kingdom
Walk alongside The Holy Spirit
For Christ did not leave us as orphans
But we act like so
His eye is on the sparrow
Are you not worthy as well?
He awaits your wait
He listens for you to listen
The kingdom of God is not in one man
But in all men

Retract your tongue from trivial things
And set it ablaze with holy praise
Do not let the deposit on your life
Be but an exchange
Fight for heaven and the glory that broke your chains
Fight for the ones that are lost
Fight to sustain those saved
This is a war for everyone's soul
Yet you've not a worry in the world?
Be ever so content where God has you
But do not let your hunger for His Spirit leave you
For when you seek Him
He will reveal Himself to you
Not just for you
But for every soul around you.
Walk with your Heavenly Father
Let His hand guide you and
Let it be known
Until the time is done
And we are home
The fire of His Spirit
Will always be shown.

R.S.

Blessed

Hello, sweet hummingbird, so small
It's been a while, since maybe last fall
I feel so blessed you came to me
Your fluttering wings are fun to see
I thank my God for sending you
Oh what a gift of green and blue.

G.S.

God's Love

Another journey will soon begin
I feel Your push and pull
I feel Your favor and Your will
Your love just makes me full
I'll rest in Your arms, so big and strong
For I know that's the place I truly belong
Right next to You as You hold my right hand
Leading me where I'll be able to stand.

G.S.

Your Gifts

As I sit in the beautiful quiet of the morning
And I look up at the glory of Your big blue sky
I'm so much in awe of the gifts that You give
Your baskets are full of such a supply
May I always be bold to tell of Your story
And lead them to Your unending glory.

G.S.

Just Ask

Holy Spirit up above
I seek Your guidance and Your love
I ask for patience, rest, and peace
And for my weakness to gently cease
You are the One who gives us life
You also take away our strife
I ask You to empower me
So I can serve You heartily.

G.S.

You Hear Me

I love the way You hear me when I cannot utter a sound
When my mind won't find the words to say
They just cannot be found
But You alone, who knows my heart and all my hurts and needs
You send Your Spirit, who speaks for me
To bless and to succeed.

G.S.

Snagglepuss

The horses are readying
The steed is pushing
The buckles are tightening
The rider is preparing
The gates are buckling
The steed is galloping.
Who is preparing?
Who is listening?

The seas are ripping
The land is crying
Footsteps lifting off
Mounting is the rider
Galloping ahead
Raising the dead.
Heaven's horns sounding

Horses galloping
The skies departing.
Who is that riding?

Foundations shaking
Beams buckling
Wood splitting
Concrete withering.
Barriers are no more
Heaven is leveling the floor.
Buckles tightening
Horses crying
Jesus Christ is
done with baptizing.

R.S.

Another Day

Another day that's new from You
Another day You'll see me through
Another day I'm blessed to see
All the beauty You give to me
Another day to bask in the sun
As I gaze at the ocean and watch all the fun
Another day to sing Your praise
And so to You my hands I raise.

G.S.

I Praise

You are the One who died for me
I pray I'll always live for Thee
I long to know just what I've done and understand Your love
For who am I—how did I earn such favor from above?
I owe my life and all I have to You, my Lord and King
I love You, so with all my heart
To You I'll praise and sing.

G.S.

I Pray and Sing

I sit at the beach and admire the colors
Of many umbrellas planted here and there
I wonder how many souls are under such beauty
So many who need my prayers
I pray they look up at the sky and see
All of Your heart and all they can be.

G.S.

Ocean Blessings

Good morning, Lord—so much on my mind
My head's spinning round—I need to unwind
As I sit at Your ocean, so full of Your grace
Your blessings are many and always in this place
I get to unwrap them one at a time
And thank You for each gift as I pen another rhyme.

G.S.

To All the Special Widows

For so many wonderful years
He was my beau
But now my name has changed
They call me his "widow"
I'm not called "us" anymore
It's "me," "myself," and "I"
I long for Your sweet touch, O Lord
That allows a great big sigh
Please, O Holy Spirit, breathe in me this day
Fill me with Your love and strength
All of this, I pray.

G.S.

Focused on God

Blessed be the man who stands where there's nowhere to stand.
Blessed be the man who calls upon righteousness when there is nothing but unrighteousness around.
Blessed is the man who conquers when he sees no army.
Blessed is the man who trusts You when he feels there is no one around to trust.
Blessed be the man who pushes through walls that appear to surround.
Blessed be the man who pursues You, even though the enemy screams and shouts.
Blessed be the man who rests in You.
Blessed be the man who keeps his head up during this journey.
Bowing down in worship to our God amidst this land, blessed be that man.

R.S.

Defend and Rescue

I learned this day I'm here to defend
And help those hearts who need to depend
Depend on the ones that our God chose
To uphold the souls where weakness shows
They're in a dark place when the Spirit says
"Go rescue the needy so they will confess
So God can deliver and take sin away."
Lord, save Your people
This I do pray.

G.S.

This Place

The ocean gives me peace and rest
It brings me close to You
The waves just ripple by and by
A never-ending view
They rise … they fall … with gentleness and grace
I thank You, Lord, for giving me this place.

G.S.

My Strong Tower

My dear Lord, if today I should crumble
Please bring me to my knees and make me humble
If I am weak, please make me strong
And let me know where I belong
I need to feel that I'm enough
When I see myself, let me see who's tough
You are my King and my Strong Tower
I pray You fill me with Your power.

G.S.

Hunger and Thirst

Dear Lord, my hunger and thirst for You are never-ending
I yearn for You day and night
Wherever I look, I can see Your love
Its beauty is always in sight
Though mountains be shaken and hills go away
Your love for me will always stay.

G.S.

Share Christ

I know the world is watching
Through all my ups and downs
I pray they see the peace in me and not the sour frowns
Lord, lift my head with style and grace
So I may see Your loving face
And how You bless us one by one
Until our days are finally done.

G.S.

Holy

To whom the sky rips open for
To whom the heavens light up for
To whom eternity sings for
Holy, Holy, Holy
Is on our tongue
My Father whom I have always had
The Spirit who always comforts and guides
To what do I declare
To the One I truly fear
You are my God
You are my Helper
We think we get it
With our corrupted scepter.

Let me trust in You
Faith in You brings joys

Joys that this world strives to spoil
Yet my faith is not in this world but in You
Your Son called my name
For once, I listened
My prayer is I continue to listen
The rest of my days.
May they begin in Sh'ma
And end in Sh'ma
Let me bow down in worship
Let me bow down in fear
It is not my story here.

Let us declare
The sovereignty of God
The Holiness of God
The absolute Love of God.
He is right there
He is waiting for you
He is seeking you
He sent for you
He pleads for you
What will it take?
What will it cost?
He gave everything
For you.

"Ask and it will be given to you; seek and you will find; knock and the door will be opened to you. For everyone who asks receives; the one who seeks finds; and to the one who knocks, the door will be opened" (Matthew 7:7–8).

R.S.

Pillow of Calm

I long for the cushion that comforted Your head
When You slept through that storm
In a boat as Your bed
You told the wind, "Be quiet and still."
It obeyed Your command, for this was Your will
Oh, how I need that peace in my storm
And Your Pillow of Calm that makes me warm.

G.S.

Our Grief

Can we be free of hurt and pain
Do memories fade away
Does life revolve around this ache
We feel from day to day
This feeling draws us near and far
To those we hold so dear
We ask why do we go through this
The answer is so clear
Our grief is now a part of us
It's become our darkest friend
A friend we never asked for
Our friend until the end.

G.S.

God's Grace

Such a vast palette of colors
God graces me again
Such a beauty right before me
Here comes my spiritual pen
The Holy Spirit tells me
to seek and I shall find
His words and thoughts for me to write
As he puts them in my mind
I thank God for the ocean so blue
As he frosts it with his foam
And then I see his huge backdrop
No need for me to roam
His big blue sky just draws me in
And fills my heart with peace
I know His blessings never stop
They always will increase.

G.S.

Why

"Why?" is what I ask myself
So many questions, Lord
This little word has so much thought
It's You I'm looking toward
You want my trust along the way
You tell me to just try
It's then You'll answer everything
Even all my questions *why*.

G.S.

I Hurt

Such salty water flows from my eyes
When I think I'm doing fine
I'm going through the steps of life
Is this some kind of sign
I desire to be a happy soul
In all I say and do
But at those times when tears just fall
My heart just sees it through
I long for peace within myself to get me through each day
One day at a time is all I can do, and I'll continue to pray
I pray God heals my heart and mind, for He's the lifter of my head
I'll trust Him for that peace each night when it's time
To rest myself on my bed.

G.S.

To God

For whom can be in Your presence
Your hands rip the sky apart
Dashing of light
We dance in fear

To God be the glory
To God be the glory

My everlasting Father
The Holy Creator of my being
You see beyond what I think
And what I am feeling

To God be the glory
To God be the glory

How hungry we are
For the full story
Yet the bites we are given
We try and assume
Partial glory

To God be the glory
To GOD be the glory

Once more I say again
Once more I pray again.

R.S.

Strife

Where am I now in this place we call life?
I see myself circling in all of my strife.
Where do I go? Which way do I turn?
My mind travels one way, my heart says, "I yearn."
My tears say, "I'm dry."
Where did they all go?
And then, in an instant, they all start to flow.
I guess where I am is where I should be.
One day at a time is all I can see.
(Praying for peace and safety for all.)

G.S.

Our Fears

O Lord, please calm our deepest fear
As wind and rain come oh so near
Help all to lean on only You
When darkness comes within our view
We ask for strength to trust You more
And Your endless grace we do adore.

G.S.

Our Circle

There's a time in life when the circle starts
It's a time when we learn and grow
We form our values in our inner self
And learn life's lessons as we go
Our circle gets bigger as time goes by
With so many lives added in
We laugh, we pray, and sometimes we cry
It's such a great feeling within
How sad when our circle goes out of round
We lose loved ones one by one
But oh, what joy and blessings we've shared
When our circle was full and such fun.

G.S.

Tears

It's our turn to cry
When all we do is sigh
We look to others for prayer
But all we do is care
We reach to them with love
And ask for help from above
God says, "I'm here for you.
You need to shed tears, too.
Please know I save them all
Whether they be big or small.
My jar is as big as My heart
So don't be afraid to start."

G.S.

Look Up

When I sit here in church
And look up at the screen
I see an ocean with waves that make me feel clean
It's God showing us to lay back and rest
He says, "Look up to Me. I'll give you My best."

G.S.

Sin

Lost again
I invite her in again
Death.
All I see are empty moments, times, and places
I wonder what is this curse?
I walk in this belief
That I am worth nothing
I invite her in again and again
I have welcomed it.
My spirit wanes and troubles
Alive again
Wondering why
Wondering why.
I cannot shake the totality of my flesh
Wandering around
Holding these worthless rags

I am lost again.
Oh Holy Spirit
Lift me again, my God
I have slipped and fallen
Yet
You hold death and hell in Your hand
And by Your hand I will rise.
Blessed are You, my Father
Lead me again, Lord
Direct my paths
Direct my steps.
My God, my God
Let heaven's hymns be sung
Made anew
The old is gone
Shake off my doubt
And burn it in the fire
Build my foundation on the rock.
Dressed in white
Unto the night
Holy is
As Holy will be
Lead me, Abba
Lead me onward once again
Let heaven's glory
Be my only story.

R.S.

Time with My Lord

Lord, as I start on this journey of time spent with You
I'll sit and reflect on this beautiful view
I pray that the ocean speaks volumes to me
of Your presence and peace
O God, help me to be
Determined, not wavering but focused on You
As I drink … for I thirst to be fresh and brand-new.

G.S.

Joy and Peace

Thank You, Lord, for birds in the air
Because of You, they have no care
Oh, that I would feel so free
When I place my trust in Thee
So God, I ask for Your sweet grace
To gently bring me to that place
That place of holy joy and peace
Where I myself to You release.

G.S.

Follow Him

I feel a tugging in my heart
I know it's You, Lord, telling me to start
You speak to me in such a way
Your Spirit says, "Follow Me and pray."
I pray on paper when You call
For this is when my blessings fall
I share my blessings with all of you
So God can bless and choose you, too
So open your heart, your mind, and your soul
And say, "Here I am to reach my true goal."

G.S.

God's Peace

As we sat and we mourned over those who are gone
I looked to my side, and I saw
A tear on the sleeve of all who were near
And the pain was so new and so raw.
I pray that we'll think of the day they went home
When they looked to our Jesus above.
It's then we all knew that in heaven we find
Real peace, real joy, and real love.
So I share this with you from deep in my soul
And I know our God's peace will again make us whole.

G.S.

God Is Comfort

I thank You, God, for keeping me under Your wing
You give comfort, protection, and all You can bring
I humble myself and surrender to You
For You are my Wonderful Counselor—it's true
Your love makes me strong in so many ways
You're my loving God
My Ancient of Days.

G.S.

The Holy Trinity

Others may love you
Others may hurt you
Others may serve you.
But I am the only One who frees you
From you.

R.S.

Think, Pray, Trust

As I sit by the ocean, my mind travels far
It brings me to places just sitting in the car
I think of the past with laughter and tears
Then I think of the future with doubt and some fears
I know God will bring me down His path, not mine
For His will is perfect
I'll trust Him to shine.

G.S.

My Bright and Morning Star

I long to always put You first
With all my heart and soul
You've always quenched my deepest thirst
And helped me to feel whole
So at this special time of year, there's one thing I must do
I'll lift You high above all else and raise my hands to You
For all You've done and all You are
You are my Bright and Morning Star!

G.S.

Holy Spirit Gives Smiles

Thanks for waking me this day
with a smile on my face
I'm filled with Your Holy Spirit
right here in my sacred place
I'm overflowing with Your Grace
I don't know what I did
But I know You're right here with me
so to You, my love I bid.

G.S.

Push Through the Puddles

Life is a puddle with ripples galore
We push and we stomp and we always make more
At times it's calm and at times it's a mess
It helps us to try and get rid of our stress
This puddle's from God—He wants us to see
Our life as a ripple, just trust Him and see
He'll give you still waters when all's said and done
And blessings will flow from Him one by one.

G.S.

God's Answers

As I sit here this day to spend time with my Lord
I read and I pray so we're in one accord
Sometimes I ask, "Where are You now?"
And then, in that moment, God shows me how
I gaze at my window, and what do I see?
A woodpecker knocking and looking at me
I smile and I laugh at God's quick reply
And I thank Him for the happy tear in my eye.

G.S.

שְׁמַע

Seek the voice of God
He loves you and those around you
Ripples on soft river streams
Fish swimming ever so gently
The Lord's hand will draw you near
Trust in Him
Trust in Him
For time evaporates
As quick as sand.
Trust our Creator
And His eternal plan.

R.S.

www.ingramcontent.com/pod-product-compliance
Lightning Source LLC
LaVergne TN
LVHW020426070526
838199LV00004B/290